Heart of Gold

Copyright © Raquel Genae Flores. All rights reserved.

Cover & Publication Designer: *Pema Siddhi*
Editor: *Brittany Priore*

Independently Published by Author
www.raquelgenae.com

ISBN 978-0-578-74692-0

For those who can see
For those who wake up & believe
For those who love so fiercely

...

⟵ ═ *Inside the Heart* ═ ⟶

01
·· THE SONNETS OF SELF-LOVE ··
*love letters; the honest stages
of loving the body & self*

33
·· RIOTING THROUGH ·· THE STREETS OF REJECTION
a tapestry of loss, rebellion, & neglect

54
·· CONNECTING THE ·· DOTS OF CHILDHOOD
tracing back to the beginning

73
·· THE LOVER & THE LOTUS ··
*a transformational journey
from romance to redemption*

98
·· HANDS OF HEALING ··
*the first steps of dealing,
healing, & peeling*

121
·· BUTTERFLIES BEYOND ··
THE BREAKDOWN
omens of growth & guidance

139
·· MIRROR, MIRROR ··
ON THE WALL
who is the most capable of them all?

156
·· THE WOMAN WHO ··
BIRTHED THE REVOLUTION
*her existence is an act of resistance—
it all starts with her*

184
·· THE TALE OF THREE EYES ··
seeing through the eyes of the divine

·· THE SONNETS OF SELF-LOVE ··

*love letters; the honest stages
of loving the body & self*

HEART • OF • GOLD

What do you love most about yourself?

The way I transmute.
That I am this ever-changing aura
of light with no form.

It is the way everything I touch turns to *gold*.

RAQUEL ✦ GENAE ✦ FLORES

Body—I am listening.

My inner child says;

What about me?
Am I not appealing enough to be admired?
Am I not tenacious enough to be looked up to?
Am I not witty enough to be heard?
What about me?

I give her all the love and praise she needs.
I comfort her for all the times that she was never seen.

Walk into my bedroom
Take a glance at the bedsheets of my wounds.

Open up my closet
Let your eyes scan the hangers of shedding skin.

Show you my backyard
looks like a graveyard
with the people I've lost to get here.

Right here
loving every inch of myself.

My beauty
runs deep
in the wells
of the temples
I have built inside

The inner architect
swells with humility & pride

I have always been told that I am too much.

Too wild to be tamed.
Too feisty to be calmed.
Too strong to belong.

I have always been told I am a lot.

I am a lot.
I am an entire universe with a vortex that can suck you in and swallow you whole in the matter of seconds.
I am the mystifying depth of the sea and I assure you even the strongest swimmers will drown in my current.
I am a lot of tough terrain and soft satin.
I am a lot of hunger. I am a lot of hope. I am a lot of adventure.
I am a lot of eccentric enthusiasm with every eruption.
The pearl beyond all your presumptions.
I am too much of the most vulnerable, exposing,
raw moments all compiled into;

One *Body*, One *Mind*, One *Soul*.

She had brunch with her angels
and treated her shadows for tea.
She honored her light
and dark
for they deserved
love
equally.

Self-sabotage feels like never having enough of yourself
for yourself

It is like getting hand-me-downs of your own energy
Scavenging to find scraps of your own time
Scraping the bowl to see if there is enough love for you

It shows in little ways
It comes and goes

Day by day

HEART + OF + GOLD

You don't have to, you know.

You don't have to live within the walls of limitations.
You don't have to live how you were told.
You don't have to be anything than what you already are.
You can be free.
You can be you
now
& know
That is enough.

I have come to realize that there is nothing more beautiful than witnessing someone in full honesty. Utterly present in deep sensitivity. Profoundly free. Uncensored—in all their entirety.

You never taught me love,
only showed me the absence of it.
Your mistakes showed me
how important it was to love myself.
And for that, I am grateful.

How cruel
I have been
to my
self

Denying her beauty
Depriving her needs
Starving her pleasures

I have broken her
down
to crumbles

Yet still
she finds a way
to be
whole
again

A flaw is a gift.

RAQUEL • GENAE • FLORES

Where did you get it?
Where did you look?
Can I buy it?
Can I find it in a book?
Can I search in a car?
Is it in the planets and the stars?
Where can I go?
Can I climb high?
Can I duck low?
Is it something you're supposed to know?
Is it in my hair?
Is it really that rare?
Is there a key?
Is it something I can see?
Will I find it if I start to drink tea?
Please, help me.
It is something I really wanna be.
Why My Dear, who told you it wasn't right here?
See look, right behind your ear!
I cannot give it to you.
It is something that you open up and cultivate.
Happiness is being your own soulmate.
A state of being you create.
An acceptance you celebrate.
The good news is
You can start at any time.
It is already inside.
Use your heart's eyes.
Your core is your prize.

Look—
Look out your window
Look at you
Look up
Look for all the little things that are sacred to you

I am tired
of seeing myself
in everyone else's
eyes
but my own.

All I want
is for my mind
to be mine
to own.

When feelings arise—I let them be. I allow them to exist. I listen closely, so I can hear what they have to say. And then, I show them the door, thank them for their visit, and let them know they can no longer stay.

When you aren't nourishing yourself

The slightest bit of time is too much
Even the smallest favor is too big
Conversations are too draining
Sounds are too loud
Tasks are too overwhelming
Exhausted becomes the new norm
Emotions flaring
Dragging you into the storm
You formed
Commanding you to transform

Beloved body,
Thank you for all that you have done. All the battles you have won. Thank you for holding me up when I wanted to collapse. Thank you for staying together when my heart wanted to fall in my lap. We have gotten so close over the years and I feel like this is just the beginning of my deep appreciation for you.
I haven't always treated you well, but I want you to know
I am now here to take care of you.

Overworked
Underpaid
Overexerted
Undersaved

Always giving it all away
Never preserving it for myself
Never letting it serve something else

I had to learn when not to speak
When to savor a moment to keep
A small moment
A small jewel
for me

*We can see the beauty in others in a matter of moments
yet take a lifetime to see the same beauty in ourselves*

When you begin to do out of love, rather than for love,
a shift occurs;

your sentences become mantras,
your thoughts become manifestations.

When you speak in love,
your words become tiny prayers tickling tummies of those
you've touched.

When you move in love,
every cell in your body is in euphoric sync,
a speck of cosmic dust drizzles every time you blink.

When you create in love,
you become a bouquet of blessings.

When your intention is to love,
you offer the world a piece of the paradise you've been
nurturing.

What a joy it is
To hear my own silence

Every second is sweet

How fascinating is it
That there are so many versions of myself
I am yet to meet

NEVER GIVE UP

ON THE INNER EXPERIENCE

YOU KNOW YOU DESERVE

We accept this idea of conditionality
Conditional love
Conditional kindness
Conditional giving
Only to those who are "deserving"
This idea
If we live up to this worthiness, then we may receive
You are deserving even at your lowest
You are worthy even at your worst
Love is unconditional
You don't need to explain why or how
You just do
This love is past due
You have been waiting years on the beauty and love
I see when I take one look at you

Be so busy adoring your life and arranging your blessings that you don't need to bend for those who don't fit in the bigger picture. Be so attentive to the way your body feels when you feed it with nutrients that it outweighs every narrow image that society says you need to be. Normalize and prioritize your pleasure. Be so passionate about your purpose that petty conversations no longer reserve a place in your life. Your strong sense of worth attracts wholeness. Someone can only add value to the experience you've already created for yourself. Be so occupied thanking those who clap that it doesn't even cross your mind about those who don't. Pay attention to the ones who do show up. The ones who do attend. The seats that are full. The hearts that spill over with no end. The ones who have come and the ones that have come to stay. A life that is full will only attract more. What you choose to focus on is what you are asking for.

I am falling more in love with my nature

My humanness
My fragility
My scars

When I can see the humanness in me
I can accept the humanness in all of who I see

May you kindle the flame of romance in your own home.

May you stuff your pillows with pleasure of everything you love the most.

May you swell in delight with every delicious detail when surrounded by all you hold close.

May you overflow with trust and tranquility of making things happen on your own time.

May your walks spring into prances
lighthearted songs and midnight dances.

May you set foot in the greatest love affair you have ever known.

May you realize that the greatest love affair is that of your own.

When you see me—
Rooted in my power
Owning my sexual nature
Embracing my divine presence
Let it be known
It is eternal
It is my ancestors
Coming through space and time
Speaking up through me
When I put my dreams first
It is for all of my lineage
Who were not afforded to dream
In their lifetime
When I laugh
My voice echoes
The joy
My ancestors feel
To see me here
I am their miracle
They dance by the bonfire
As I overcome

Choosing to love myself is the greatest honor I can give.
My beauty has layers. My sexiness is expansive.
My fire burns and I have no intention of ever watering myself down.

A lot of this new found love came from unlearning
Unlearning the wildfire of anger
Learning to hose myself down with *compassion*
Unpacking the boxes of guilt
Moving into a new home of *empowerment*
Unwriting the narratives of self-hate
Rewriting my own novels of *self-love*
Unweaving the strands of shame
Sewing my own blankets of *appreciation*
Unlearning my fears that were never really mine
Learning how to be love again
Vibrating higher where my true self emerges
A place within myself where my heart is *aligned*

Breathe into every morning.
Remind yourself of everything you are.

You are loved.
You are understood.
You are forgiven.
You are beautiful.
You are strong.
You are important.

What you say matters. What you do counts. You have time.
Touch as many hearts as you can.

Change begins with you.

·· RIOTING THROUGH ··
THE STREETS OF REJECTION

a tapestry of loss, rebellion, & neglect

To all my misfits:

My beautiful catalysts
you will heal from all of this.
You were born to shake shit up.
Don't let them bury your gift.

They aren't mad at you.
They are mad at themselves.
Because you are the truth.
You shine light on the darkest crevices of their being.
...And that's why my darling, they will never like you.

You are a reminder of everything they haven't faced yet.

I thought maybe if I wore this mask long enough
They would love me
And they did

I never felt more alone

I sat
Huddled up
In the corner of the bedroom closet
Of myself

Peeping through the panels
Hands wrapped
Over my knees

Waiting
Hoping
Thinking

That maybe one day
I could come out as just me

That maybe If I showed all of me
I could be someone to love, too

You can be painted as a monster
when they are afraid of the dark

If only they turned
on the light

They would see
it was
only
their own shadow

I promise you that rejection is protection from all that is not meant for you.

I know it hurts.
I've begged to be in spaces I don't belong.
I've looked for a safe haven in all those who couldn't love me.

But the universe is never wrong. It sees better for you even when you don't see better for yourself.

When someone goes out of their way to make you feel unimportant
        it is because you are *that* important.

You have to know just how brilliant you really are.
Have you felt the gravitational pull of your spirit? The way everything around you collapses without needing much of anything? That your fingertips and lightning have something in common—the staggering shock of one simple touch. Your skin is electric. Your passion sends chills down spines. Your intensity is eye-opening. Efforts to diminish you only show how voluminous you
        truly are.

If my truth offends you...I'm not sorry.
I've spent too many years apologizing for my existence.
—Met with so much resistance.

I had to let their opinions fall away like leaves
I had to let them hold onto their version of me

That they created
Often outdated
      Often miscalculated
           Often a representation
                Of all their trauma

Creating past suffering & self-induced drama
Long enough to distract them from what's hurting inside
Never putting down their pride and always looking to be identified

Let the pain of the world crumble at your feet.
Sometimes
You are too smart, too beautiful, and too much of
Everything
That it scares people who do not feel enough.

I've lost friends
For being introduced to their friends
As if we can't all connect
As if we can't all win
I've lost friends
Who were never really friends
Only people who didn't want others to see—*my light within.*

If you want
I can be the bad guy
You can say I'm the reason why
You can refuse to take the lessons

You can cover your ears
When class is in session

But I will continue to come back
Like a boomerang
Until you level the frame
& see the recurring lessons are yours to claim

Understand that not everyone will be able to receive you.

Not everyone is ready to receive you.
Not everyone is meant to receive you.

Stop forcing it.
Leave them alone.
Go live your life, Earth Angel.

Sometimes, you get caught in the crossfires of their self-hate.

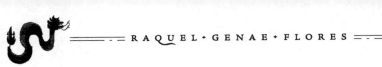

I couldn't be
who they wanted me to be.
I choose me.

I choose me.
In sickness.
In health.
& even in death
We never part.

They threw bricks at me
So I built a home

They neglected me
So I could realize how I've neglected myself

They joined forces to try to make me feel weak
But I only grew stronger

They tried to block the way to my blessings
Only so I could find a new way

They tried to blind me
But all it did was help me see

That on a planet of billions of people
there is nothing that feels better
than just being me

Massive hearts become massive threats
here to disrupt
the fragile collective slumber of the masses.

I was everything you never wanted.
I showed you all the parts of yourself that you hated.
I reminded you of what you could never accept.

But I was your greatest gift,
I was everything your soul needed.

Ba ba black sheep
Won't you come out and play?
Your wool as dark as night
Your heart as light as day

The whole world could turn their back on you,
but make sure you never turn your back on yourself.

What I really want to say is—thank you.

Thank you for never seeing my genius and allowing me to see the genius in myself. Thank you for inspiring me to love harder, to overflow.

While others waded above
I traveled below.

Down there,
I found wisdom for all of my woes.

Thank you for the depth and the teachings I needed to know.

Thank you.

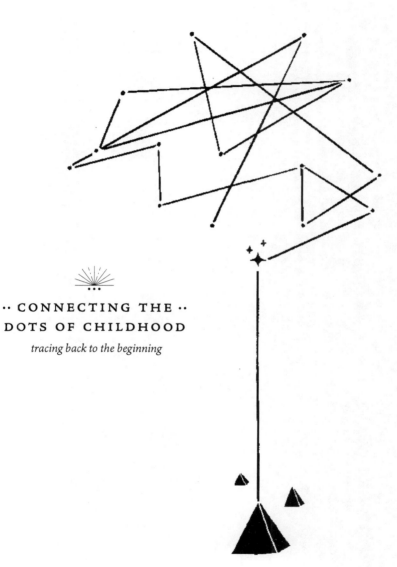

·· CONNECTING THE ··
DOTS OF CHILDHOOD

tracing back to the beginning

As a child
I would find
the hidden riches in every place we went.
I would enter abandoned homes and hearts of the broken
and discover mounds of treasure.

And, somehow, I still find myself doing that.

A little scavenger of magic
A treasure hunter
Finding all the beauty
in the forgotten, neglected, and mistreated.

Collecting shells of sorrow
and giving them love
Reminding them
in my arms, they will always have a place to shine.

I cherish you
You are gold to me
Something I cannot find anywhere
A rare beauty, with every wear & tear

a mother's love

She used her thick, dark hair to sew quilts
So she could take us on picnics at the park
Grazing ducks and passing monarchs
I was her greatest dream
In full manifestation
Even if the edges of my cliffs scared her
The universe dared her to free fall
With a mind so open
And a heart so free

You could drink her divinity and swear,
this is what the world has been missing.

She is the remedy.

I almost died in Spain
I almost changed my name
I almost became a lawyer
I almost moved to Argentina with my father
I almost didn't write this book
One choice was all it took

All these almosts led me to here
No regrets and no longer living in fear

I believe that a "bad kid" is never really bad
they are a manifestation of energy
a host for their parent's pain
brought here to teach a lesson

They are here to teach about love
A blessing in disguise
If one has the eyes
for it

Carrying heavy history from the past
The offering of the outcast
Parents whisper around the room
Only looking to have their egos groomed

Leaving a child—with no guidance on how to bloom

HEART OF GOLD

He was not only a boy, but a butterfly

I wish somebody would have told him that he was not only a boy, but a *butterfly*.

I grew up
watching him
pick apart his wings

I grew up
watching him
take lessons from the wrath of kings

He would deny it but
you would find him in gardens
instead of boxing rings

I wish somebody would have told him that he was not only a boy, but a *butterfly*.

That he didn't have to hide himself away
That there could be a safe space for him to stay
That his natural essence didn't have to cause a war
That his femininity was something to adore
An avenue to explore

I grew up
watching
until I could not
stand
to watch no more

I wish somebody would have told him that he was not only a boy, but a *butterfly*.

I wish he knew that the ones who were beating him down
were begging
I wish he knew
it was his wings they were crying for

It is one thing to have a sister
A sacred feminine bond intertwined in history

It is quite another to have
A sister
And a spirit guide
In one

                    Now, that is—magic.

I was told the way I talked was wrong

The way I walked was wrong
If I expressed, it was wrong
If I was depressed, it was wrong

Spent so many years trying so hard to be right
Only to understand that I never had to fight
for love

When I was 8,

My parents brought home a swing set

I spent my days with beaming sun rays
While giant, green grasshoppers cheered me on

My swing would kick up the dirt
Grinning—as the soles of my feet reach for the sky
Even when the swing set would shake
I never thought about falling
Only hoping, one of my toes would get stuck in a cloud

No matter how high the swing
Or how explosive the jump

My feet always landed on the ground.

I have always been my mother's protector and my sister's keeper

Made sure to keep them out of harm's way
If anyone had something to say
They would have to answer to me
They were not my children
But they gave me a mother's anxiety

I couldn't let the world crush their gentle nature
A nature I knew nothing about
A presence so pure
I guarded them with my life
My two babies of light

I failed to see
How my hardness hurt them
How my callous and controlling ways betrayed them
How my fire lit up their skin and forced them to run into a den
Not knowing when it would be safe to come out again

All along,
Who they really needed protection from
Was
The carnivorous aspects of me

Maybe I wanted someone to stay

I was a little girl
When my world was swept away
So many countries
So many schools
In a blink of an eye
So many hellos
So many goodbyes

I wanted someone there
I clung onto you in the chaos of uncertainty
All I wanted
Was
One thing
In my life
To

       Stay

You treat my body like it's something to hide
Like a threat to other women
And a way to increase another man's pride

An instrument to dim another's shine
Somehow a distraction from their time

As if it is a weapon
To be concealed
To feel ashamed for the uncomfortability
You make others feel

our house
was more like
an open field
where
we let our demons
run wild

no boundaries
no walls
only a battlefield
we saw it all

I was never really called pretty
Stronger than most kids my age

Big brown hands
Big brown feet

I was too loud for my own good
I liked to roll around and play fight
There was nothing soft about my spunk
Nothing sweet about my feisty funk

Later on
I had to realize I was my own kind of pretty
Maybe not the kind of pretty that you see in movies
But the kind that had a valiant heart that people made movies about

Maybe like a superhero
And being strange was my superpower

They say

I have your carefree spirit
Your almond eyes
Strong legs
Nurturing hips

You taught me to give
Taught me to give with no expectations
Taught me how to be selfless
So much that I became less of my self

So much that I said yes when I wanted to say no
So much that I stayed when I wanted to go

I used to tell you
You remind me of the children's book
The Giving Tree
But now I remember
All that was left
Was its trunk

-taking care of myself first is the biggest gift I can give to others

I am no victim
Got my Daddy's rage
My Mama's guilt
The cycle ends here

I am no victim
Grew up too fast
Survived
Walls too high to get past
But now I am ready to thrive

I am no victim
I was the scapegoat for your suffering
Held you accountable
With no sugarcoat or buffering

I am no victim
I see through the veil
Not into this conditioned fairytale
I am no product of the system

In the moments when

my blood boils
I grind my teeth
Fists clenched
on the verge of blacking out

I remember my ancestors
that I have been entrusted to transcend
Feeling the aid my angels send
I feel the push and pull of my ego and spirit

I am here to choose differently
My anger listens to me
I am here to liberate my lineage
Disengage with the routine of rage
& let my eternal self turn the page

The elderberry tree

There was an elderberry tree
it stood tall
in my backyard
always available to me

I passed it many times
without seeing
Seasons went by
without awareness of its being

I left
without ever savoring a berry

Later on,
I wondered what it would
be like
to stand in the presence
of this rarity

Not knowing—that for years
the tree was in plain sight
but the time wasn't right

A reminder
that I was never lost
only hazy in memory
I simply swallowed the key

Just like the elderberry tree
the answers have always been available to me

Talking about your trauma and expressing the ways your parents impacted you is not being ungrateful. You don't need to justify every single thing that happened. It takes fearlessness to be this vulnerable. It takes a new level of love for yourself and your family to set out to do this kind of work. You are not only healing yourself but also future generations to come.

...It is because I love you so much that I am willing to bear naked honesty. It is because I love you so much that I am bringing your attention to the behavioral patterns that have been passed down to me. It is not to hurt you, it is so I can deepen our love, our connection. I only want to uplift us, but part of uplifting is being able to see everything that is weighing us down. Seeing what we don't want to see. I am willing to look at it. Feel it. Let it pass through me and I am strong enough to let it go.

...The truth is uncomfortable, and I am prepared to sit with the uncomfortable. I talk about trauma not because I want to blame you but because I love you enough to bring this authentic accountability to the table. It is because I love you that I want to share this awareness with you—this place of learning.

It is to hold your hand as we go beyond the fear and arrive at a place of true love and empowerment.

·· THE LOVER & THE LOTUS ··

*a transformational journey
from romance to redemption*

Early morning—the sunlight peeks through the corner of the window, illuminating my supple breasts. The outline of my hips are his horizon. My skin is his cinnamon.

The curtains whistle as he begins to press the cool tip of a paintbrush on my back. He fills my flesh with hues of nature. In the smooth dance of my playful curiosity I ask, "What is it that you are painting?"

He responds with a soft smile—a lotus.
I never understood how a lotus survived in the most unbearable conditions. Their resilience, unmatched for even time herself. A beauty favored by the gods. Even at all odds, nothing could stop her rebirth. None of it made sense—until I met you.

You have blessed my life
In ways you might never understand

You have dug up my weeds
Placed them on display for the world to see

You uprooted my pain
You gave me knowledge
You gave me the growth I asked for
That sat there on my plate

You impacted me in ways
You never wanted to
But all I do is learn by you

Trigger teacher
You have showed me the way
You have taught me how to choose to see a brighter day

He asked me,
"What do you like?"
"How can I please you?"
As he ran his fingers across unexplored land.

I stuttered.
I shamed him for not knowing.

But the truth is—I didn't know either.
I didn't know my body.
I didn't know myself.

We find comfort in forever.
We find reassurance in hearing,
"...I'll never leave"

But what if we decided to create a nest of nourishment in now?
What if we found joy in knowing that everything changes?
What if our love for growth outweighed our need for control?

    What if we *welcomed* letting go?
...That our days of sprouting could soothe
                              all the nights of doubting.

You use words like
Should
Supposed to
Have to

I wonder who
Placed such heavy expectations
On you

And if
Your shoulders
Are weary of carrying them

I broke my own heart
Before you ever did
Still recovering from
Replaying imaginative scenarios

I hurt my own feelings
Before you ever had the chance to
Impulsive reactions was only a fraction
Of what my distracted mind could do

My expectations crushed me
Before your actions could
Maybe I thought
You would
Save me from my own destruction

When someone says they care—pay attention to how they care.
Care does not roll off the harsh tongue.
Caring is not controlling.
It is not co-dependent nor critical.
Caring is not yelling at the top of your lungs with lazy judgement. It does not blurt out backhanded compliments. Care is not dismissive. When they say they care, watch how they care. Feel how they care. Your heart will know when you are being cradled or cut down. Don't let people stamp care on their own inability to assess their feelings and manipulate you into thinking this is what care looks like.

You keep asking for a fresh start

Like as if you can erase what has been done
Like as if relationships are all just fun

You are always avoiding the work
The self work
That could make us work

—Love is

When their smell runs up your nose like a spice of nostalgia
When you have seen them before
But you can't quite put your finger on it
Their presence feels familiar
The kind of familiar that
When you look in their eyes
You see many lifetimes
They taste like divine timing and universal outlines

And then
It hits you all at once
Love is
Returning home to everything you have ever known

It is not what they did
It is how they did it

    That shows you the frequency they emit

You don't have to morph into your partner's wants and needs.
You are not a playlist of their interests.
You are not a dictionary of their sayings.
You are not a manual of their mannerisms.

Make sure to be yours, first.
Have your own hobbies.
Curate your own music taste.
Create your own style.
Take yourself on your own dates.

Want you, first.
Be confident in the cultivation of your own life.

I didn't know that my love had been selfish
That loving you was really about me
I didn't love myself
I needed more from you

me, me, me

        I loved you the only way I knew how

But I learned
I studied
I grew

To love in the way you needed to be loved
 Not how I wanted to love you

I learned how to love from a firefly

I chased it down
In the middle of the night
Its luminescent bulb was swirling in the midnight sky

I quickly clasped it in my fist so I could take a peek
with one eye open I look into the cusp of my hands

The firefly sings with a light that even the sleeping sun can hear
gold trickles down my fingertips

A gentle voice escapes from the joining of my palms
I press my ear close
> "You must let me go. I will not last long if you capture me."

> "But you're the only firefly I have seen. What if I never see you again?

> "Open your eyes. There are millions of us hidden in the trees. All you have to do is come to the forest to find me. Open your hands and trust me—you will see."

I bite my lip in impulsive belief and set the firefly free.
As he flies away, one by one, the trees gleam like ornaments.

That night, the forest lit up for me.

The pain to outgrow
To know something nobody knows
To torture yourself to stay
To avoid the day
Where you have to face the truth
Roll up your sleeves
Squeeze out the juice
Of what we once had
Walking away with a bucket of memories
Broken
        But glad

You see, the presence of love does not make you feeble. Love doesn't make you small or insignificant. No, not at all. Love is a fortress of all the forces inside of you. Love is all encompassing, gulping down all other realities—setting fire to all that is untrue. It is unannounced and unapologetic. The feeling of increasing speed as your heart starts to race—a flash of fear. We yank the steering wheel, trying to control the drive. Love is not scary. We are scared that love can make us feel this...*alive*.

Losing you was like
Losing all my limbs

Losing you was like
Learning to walk again

Losing you was like
Dying from the inside out
Tumbling into a pit
where no one could hear me

Not a scream
Not a shout

you touched a chord inside of me
I looked into you
all I could see was
mirrors

—you are my deepest reflection

I never realized
How much
I talked down to you
Always tried to negate the words you said

Reminded you of how much you didn't understand
Because you were a man

You could never taste my wounds
Or know my experience
So I made you wrong for it
Throw tantrums and fits
I ask myself
Where did I learn this?
Who have I been trying to prove myself to?

I see my dad in you
All the times I was belittled
And, now I'm here
Belittling you

I'm not sure if
You will ever see me
For me

You are far too busy
Playing tapes
In your head
Of who I used to be

And the most heartbreaking part of it all—was to see how little I cared for myself. How desperate I was for you to complete me. How badly I needed you to see me. How much I pleaded for your lungs in my own breath. How I wanted to be your wife more than I wanted my own life.

I was a *dangerous* lover.
Ready to give my absolute all to that one person.
You could even say I was a bit of a hopeless romantic.
Someone who would wait years for a glimpse of potential,
just some sort of change to prove my intuition wrong.
Anything. Always looking for that sliver of hope to hold on to.

Then, I fell into a different kind of love. A flame that burned with the same ferocity. I found the kindest love inside of him. He softened even the volcanic crust of my core.

Falling in love taught me that my love was an open field with infinite acres. It wasn't measurable and it wasn't going anywhere. I created this love. I had all the ingredients. He cracked open my heart so wide that I found love in all things.

The kind of love that soars. Love that rises like steam after a shower—seeping out of your pores. Love that laces your lungs with the breath of life.

He opened the flood gates of my soul and showed me that love wasn't just about him. It was in all ways—always.

I became a lover of living fully, utterly open with my whole and attentive heart.

I became a hopeless romantic for humanity and that will never change.

I want them to know I have enough love *for us all.*

I want my family to know there is a future in our flaws. That we never had to know it all. Being a real model has served me more than fulfilling a role. That the power of heart and soul will always win over control. With a little bit of attention and willingness to learn, we can enjoy our harvest and tend to our ferns.

I have enough love *for us all.*

I want my friends to know that I want their growth like my own. Our sisterhood has been my sanity. You inspire me to live louder, demand more, and feel safe in my skin. I have been a sponge to your love and support. Thank you for the lives you bless and allowing me to rest.

I have enough love *for us all.*

I want my lovers to know I am full of gratitude for every moment you broke me, stroked me, and provoked me. The mirrors of self-reflection guided me to the dissection and connection of my truest self.

I have enough love *for us all.*

I want anyone who has ever helped me or hurt me to know they were a sacred teacher who served me so vigilantly by being themselves. I keep our memories like I keep books— up on bookshelves.

I have enough love *for us all.*

You can keep burning
Destroying
Polluting
But I will continue to grow back
Even more luscious than before

Just like the earth
I have enough love *for us all.*

maybe love was less about receiving what I thought I wanted

and more about becoming what I always needed.
the soulmate,
the friend,
the parent—

was always me.

·· HANDS OF HEALING ··
*the first steps of dealing,
healing, & peeling*

The Big Ugly Truth

The truth is—healing can be gut-wrenchingly painful. It isn't cute or sparkly or neat. It is the kind of change that makes everyone squirm in their seat. Acceptance can be like pulling teeth. It isn't just the bubble baths, masks, and matcha tea.

Seeing yourself without filters, good lighting, and an edited lifestyle isn't always pretty.

With real pain comes real joy.

I believe many of us are only half ass living...half ass excited, half ass sad, half ass motivated...when we repress our emotions, we protect ourselves. But we also block the opportunity of real happiness. We stop ourselves from experiencing the full spectrum of emotion.

You will cry. You will scream. You will want to rip your hair out. You will feel like your insides are on fire. You will feel as if it will never end. You will beg for the healing to stop. You will feel broken beyond repair. It will feel like everything is falling apart. You will bite your tongue, hoping to swallow it. Chew your nails off while being stripped of everything you thought you knew.

And then, you will start to see a speck of light. You feel a small change inside. Then you fall. Get back up. Fall. Get back up. In whatever the weather, you fight for yourself within the dark abyss of all the things that have happened to you.

As you train, you practice. That weight becomes lighter. Your days start to feel a little brighter. Not because anything happened...but because you've changed and that makes all the difference. You've lost so much, only to have gained yourself. Something about you radiates. That healing glow permeates.

& in my sadness
I found stillness
& in my stillness
I found my power.

I always thought strength was how tough I could be. How I could whip out my voice in an unbreakable tone. I thought it was being solid as stone. I thought it was being stiff in my comfort zone. I was taught strength was doing it all on my own. That it was demanding. Commanding the ceilings & swallowing the skies. I had a fear of letting anyone see me shed a tear. I hid behind the word strong as a way to be brutal in my blunt honesty. I worked my gifts against me. I mirrored this idea of strong for so long until it led me into a wall, and I realized this is not being strong at all. So many walking around with hardened shells, calling it strong. Justifying the chip on their shoulder as a symptom of getting older. Strength is not needing to be right. Strength is not always ready to fight. Strength is not abusive. Strength is stepping into the light. I took all the notes. I studied the ones before me closely. Then, I graduated. I reached a strength I had not known. An island I had never been to. I started to witness my strength evolve. I started to use my words as tools to solve. To help. To love. I started to see that strength was softly reaching out my hand with a kindness I never thought I was worthy of. Strength is remembering all the times the universe has shown you grace and bringing that same grace to every interaction. It is feeling the connection of precious life around you and letting love be your reaction.

I was waiting for you
to see
the god you are meant
to be

Being a healer is being a warrior
It is not delicate
It takes insurmountable strength to move forward
It is doing the work
For yourself
For others
For the collective of human consciousness

I spent the week in Mexico and was on a plane ride back home to Miami. A woman sat down next to me. Her long chestnut hair swooped around me as she took her seat and filled the plane with warmth. You could tell that generosity was her first nature. She looked over at me and offered me anything sweet she could find in her purse and I kindly accepted. We immediately started talking about our lives and she mentioned how in love she was. She spoke about all the romantic dates & flirting with fate. Yet, still she hesitates. She expressed her long history of abusive relationships and a deep fear of being hurt again—unsure how to fully trust and love again. Exclaiming she gives so much love to others and all she wishes is for God to bring her someone who will love her the way she loves. As her eyes swell with tears, she manages to say, "When will God send me the person who is going to make me happy and love me?" Our eyes locked and there was a silent pause between us. I gently touched her hand. "God has already given you that person. That is you. You are the love of your life and only you can truly make yourself happy. God wants to give you everything your heart desires, but you must feel worthy first. You must heal in order to receive." In that moment, up in the air, we were suspended in time. Higher dimensions were at play and a supreme being was at work to deliver both of us a message. I looked right in the eyes of my past self and I reassured her it would be okay; she would be okay. This wasn't goodbye. She will always be a part of me. At one point, I needed her. She needed me. But it was finally time to part ways,

peacefully.

Forgive yourself for all the times you've settled.
Forgive yourself for all the times you convinced yourself you deserved less.

Forgive yourself for all the times you thought love was constantly fighting.
Forgive yourself for hiding.

Forgive yourself for falling into the temptations of false inviting.
Forgive yourself once, twice, and however many times you need to be here in the moment
inciting
a
change.

Your legacy starts with where it hurts the most.
It starts with addressing how you treat the people closest to you.
It starts with what you keep avoiding and what's the hardest to do.
That's where your legacy lies.
Start there.

Do what gives back to your life.
Foods that give back to your body.
Connections that ignite your soul.
Conversations that feed your mind.
Actions that are aligned.

We expect pain to look soft
merciful tears begging us for help

But pain can show up
As rage
As cruelty
Laughing at others
Brittle judgment

Pain has so many faces
So when faced with it
Show them a power that pain is no match for
Spill over the kind of love the angels sing out for

HEART + OF + GOLD

The more I hustle
The more I heal.
The more I climb
The more I reveal.

The hustle
The healing

Are intertwined.

Because when I reach a mountaintop,
I want to be able to taste the wind.
I want to feel the sunset baking my skin.

I want to feel every single vibration these heights take me.
I want to know what it's like to see what these struggling nights make me.

I am letting go
Letting go of the programming
Letting go of the need for control
Letting go of what I feel like others stole

I am letting go of all the burden
I picked up
And have yet to set down
I am letting go of all the noise in the background

HEART + OF + GOLD

In a fast society where hate is being served on the menu. When being negative is the normalized thing to do. When hurting someone is as easy as pulling through a drive-thru. Fear on all the screens and everybody is afraid of being seen. Taking tolls to the

soul.

Remember to take the long way home. Remember that you can cook your own recipes and be the first to roam. Remember that hands that hurt can also heal. Remember we are looking for a way to express how we really feel. Remember you have the power to change the channel and show the world what it is to be real.

The more I don't take it personal

The

More

Room

I

Have

For

Peace.

HEART OF GOLD

I have been on both sides
The bully and the bullied
Spat insecurities out of my immature mouth
Been cut by the cruel words of others
Left and been left
Passed and failed tests
A goddess of the illuminated
A priestess of all that is hidden and hated

What I have learned is

Masking pain is a losing game
We all hurt and get hurt
No one wins
We place the blame on any name
But our pain is all the same

Your comfortability will not save you.
Your avoidance will not save you.
Your indifference will not save you.

Compassion is taking the time to try to understand where people are at—where they have been. It is to know the place people are speaking from.

If they are speaking from

A place of love
Or
A place of suffering

It doesn't define them
It means

That is the place
They are choosing to live in.

To all the strong friends,
The have it all together friends,
The down in any weather friends,

You don't have to be so strong all the time. You can put down the weight of the world you've been carrying on your back. It's okay, you are safe. You are always taking care of everyone else. Let someone take care of you for a change. You don't need to be doing anything. You can let down your hair. Breathe. Check on you. You don't have to keep it all together. Let it out. Cry. Slow down.
Let the Universe take it from here. Sit back.
Fall back
and trust we will catch you.

You cannot take a vacation away from yourself
You cannot take a road trip away from your negative thoughts
You cannot take a flight away from your trauma
You cannot take a cruise across oceans away from your conditioning

Your baggage is yours
It is here to stay

I pray you know everything around you is always working in your highest favor. I pray you are able to look around. See the trees bending to your grace. See the bushes bowing to your benevolence. See the sky beaming to your buoyancy as you bounce down the sidewalk. I pray you don't only know this but you go outside and feel the world's embrace. I pray you feel the universe's arms of support in your most trying times. I pray you roar in laughter as life places you on its shoulders to marvel at the magnitude of magnificence your life holds.

Let hurting catch up with them
                         as healing catches up with you.

If you are not compassionate towards those who show
no compassion
What is the difference between you and them?
Real strength is helping those who don't know how to ask for it.
Forgiving those who do not ask for forgiveness.
Loving those who don't know how to love.

In the end,
the world takes care of you since you have taken care of the world.

·· BUTTERFLIES BEYOND ··
THE BREAKDOWN

omens of growth and guidance

I urge you to chase all that calls you
Chase the intensity of your ideas
Chase your curiosity
Chase the butterflies of all your breakdowns
Chase the sound of simplicity
Chase the seeking souls
in synchronicity

Bridge the gap
Between
Who you think you are
And
Who you actually are

We are always
Working
Talking
Doing

Endlessly pursuing
Without a quiet place to come back to

Turn off the tv
Put down your phone
Close the fridge

Stop for a second
Silence the chatter
Tune out what doesn't matter

Tune into yourself
What do you hear?
What do you feel?
Listen to the story your body is *longing* to tell

You spend so much time
wanting
to be something
you *already* are.

When we want, we think we are separate from what we desire.
You are already *everything* you ask to become.

I like a lot of things
I could be a lot of things

But I knew I had grown
When my taste became
More intentional

I could like something
And put it back
I could say no
And take only
What I need

Lets talk about habits

Think about
Every thought
Every action
Every reaction

What does what you do every day reflect?
What do your impulses detect?
What patterns are going unchecked?
What is your ego trying to protect?

Interject
Redirect
Resurrect

One tiny shift creates ripples—it all connects.
The willingness to change is the fire you've already set.
The breakdown and breakthrough of the butterfly effect.

Maybe it was the righteous ego in me
Judging you by the way you judge others

The truth is—

>I am no better
>We are no different
>We are still
>Vibrating
>At the same frequency

There is no wrong choice. I know how it feels to want to do everything, that your mind scattters in such a hasty manner that it leads you to do nothing. I know how it feels when your inspiration leaves you paralyzed with indecision. I understand the ache you feel when there is so much greatness brewing inside of you & have absolutely no idea how to express it. Feeling stuck feels like dwindling away. Faking conversations on productivity. Fatigued from your pacing thoughts as time chips away at your goals. Jet lagged from your own journey.

But, I swear this feeling will not last forever. This moment is trying to teach you. A higher power is trying to reach you. What you are doing right now might not be what you want to do forever, and that's okay. You're not supposed to have it all figured out. You can change your mind. You can change your relationships. You can change your career. You can change where and how you are living. If you're going to commit to something, commit to change. Make a choice and stick to it. Make a change and breathe through it. Make your life as monumental as possible and work for it.

They will resent you for
Growing
They will try to make you feel
Guilty
For growing
As if— they don't have the same two feet
To walk alongside you

My feet kiss the earth beneath me

One, two, three, four,

I feel this stream of energy wrapped around my back
This enchanted goddess of the galaxy
Here for my protection

When I walk
She guides
Someone I can confide in
She has stretched me far
Expanded me wide

No move a mistake
Only steps to become more awake

everything you see in me is you

what you wish for is here and true

everything you see in me is you

this is the peak of your breakthrough

everything you see in me is you

all you had to do was adjust the view

everything you see in me is you

we were always one we were never two

Your past doesn't get to decide who you are
Your mistakes are your milestones
They taught you how to be better, see better, love better
Your past sharpened your discipline and fixed your focus
You learned how to say no and when it was time to let go
You discovered the little things that make your insides glow
All the needs that feed your soul
This kind of growth was always the goal
So, never stop designing your life—imperfectly
with all your desires on display
Picking up pieces along the way

Your magic is in your mess. It is what inspires—shapes you.
It is what draws people in—a reminder we are all human.

When you're feeling sad, create.
When you're feeling angry, create.
When you're feeling lost, create.

                                                        Creativity will heal us all.

You are here for a reason
What you're going through is only for a season
If you need to
Crawl back into your cocoon
Do whatever is necessary
To bloom

It is me.
It is my resistance to change.
It is my excuses.
It is my stubbornness to new ideas.
It is my fear of letting go.
It is me.

Let me turn my angst into art
Origami butterflies fluttering from the heart

"So, how's that working out for you?
Are you more *free*?"

·· MIRROR, MIRROR ··
ON THE WALL

who is the most capable of them all?

I hope you find the courage to be yourself in a crowded room. I hope you love everything you see in the mirror before you love the person lying next to you. I hope you understand that your ideas are weightless without execution. I hope you recognize your fears but let them take the backseat on the way to your dreams. I hope you know there is no light at the end of the tunnel. You are the light and you are never limited in anything you do.

So, I hope you choose to take that chance to live every single day free, wild, and doing
                                    what you fucking love.

She who wanders
Winds up
Finding her self

Celebrate yourself
Every small victory deserves to be seen
By you

Accept that compliment
Let yourself bask in the admiration
Receive all their praise
Let your days amaze you

Shake hands with yourself
Pat yourself on the back
Even when no one claps
Make that extra lap
For you

You are not a comfort zone
You are an entity all on your own

Know exactly what you want,
But surrender to how it is going to happen.

Surrender to trying to figure out every detail.
Surrender to comparison.
Surrender to impatience.

Surrender to all that is happening.
Surrender to all that is challenging.
So, life can create all you're imagining.

I see no enemy

Let us make a toast
Even in all its perplexity

I can be surrounded in a room
full of all those who have hated me
And still feel
Love

I am the feeling you get when your ears ring in ecstasy
as you hear your favorite song
I am the feeling you get when your taste buds dance
as you bite into rich food after waiting for so long

You cannot replace me
Misplace me like your keys

I am not going anywhere
Even when I'm not there physically

We speak in soliloquies
And upkeep our honey like bees

My love is a silhouette
For every woman who is not me

Princess and the Pea

"Why do you ignore me?"
When you know this is all
You truly want

"Why do you let fear take charge?"
It is these questions
That will be left to haunt

Your every thought and every move
I know you feel me
I know you ache

It doesn't matter what you say
If you are not ready to listen
You can hide from everyone
But you cannot hide from me

I am the truth
I am you
I am here to set you free

If only you learned to trust in my ability
The only fear
You should have
Is a life that is not yours
A love that is settled for

A purpose half done
Never complete
Never walking through that door
Of what could be

He said,
"One day you'll see...
You're gonna miss out"
I said,
I never miss out on what is meant for me
Even if you gain all the fame and money
I never want to be anywhere else
Than where I'm meant to be

If you are going to be a master of anything,

Be a master of peace, a teacher of patience, an artist of kindness.
Sculpt the mastery of love.

When you start to see others come out of hiding,
it creates the opportunity to step out of your own cave.

Whenever you feel like you are embarking on this journey alone,
Remember that you are allowing millions to live authentically
and reach their goals
just by being yourself.

Your vision starts to clear their doubt.
Your aspirations become their daily inspiration.
Your ambition is the engine.
Your reason becomes their stimulation.

You expand the imagination of what is possible.

When they see you do it, their dreams become palpable.
That new life becomes attainable—almost practical.
Their taste buds savor the change when stepping on the other side.

They will never forget,
You were the first one to take that stride.

I always needed more
Something I used to beat myself up for
Until it became something I couldn't ignore
This insatiable thirst for my liberation

Connecting every birthmark
Like points on a map
Sitting on the cosmos' lap
While the past, present, and future overlap

Arriving in real freedom
Welcoming
   All.

I was done forcing
Pushing
I took all that energy
And poured it
into me

I wouldn't call myself picky but more so aware.
Aware of my worth and the space I take up.
Aware enough to know where to invest my energy and
what simply isn't worth my time. I value where I'm at, the
frequency exchanges I have, and I don't waste a second of it.
I'm making maps. I'm making plans. I'm studying in libraries
searching for the rusted books that hold the keys to the universe.
I think big. I feel big. I speak big. I love big. I'm aware of how small
this society has designed us to feel. But it only makes me grow
bigger. I must be selective because I refuse to have small
conversations with a small mindset in a small life.
I simply cannot stand by when deep down my
heart knows we were destined to be so, big.

My Dear,

If there is one thing I know
If there is one thing that is clear

There is one thing
you must never apologize for
That is—
having a big heart

Do not waste another second waiting on anything or anyone.
Bet on yourself and go live happily ever fucking after.

·· THE WOMAN WHO ··
BIRTHED THE REVOLUTION

*her existence is an act of resistance—
it all starts with her*

The revolution is alive in everything you do

It is in how you think
It is in the words you speak
It is in how you dress
It is in how you express
It is in the food you eat
It is in the company you keep

It is in the way you love
With no limits
And confinements of how we've been taught
It is being able to stand on your own
Loyal to a bigger purpose
The kind of integrity that could never be bought

You are a walking revolution
A symbol of evolution
Empower yourself with every choice you make
Every risk you take

Choosing yourself is the most radical thing you could ever do
Pick yourself
And watch how everything you have ever desired comes to you

Brown skin
Powerhouse woman
With your brick thighs
Honey eyes
You have lived many lifetimes
You don't fit any size
Your mind challenging the planet to rise

There is a difference between existing and growing.
Do not be fooled by age.
Just because one has lived long, does not mean one has lived *full*.

At any age
In any stage of her life

When she is awakened
She is a goddess awakened
A deity in the making
Her reign is not to be mistaken

I see many goddesses
But a goddess awakened sees herself
She is realizing
She is actualizing

She sees her prowess in every field
Her vulnerability as her sword
Not her shield
I have a special place in my heart
For a goddess awakened and revealed

The voice in your head is not yours
It came from somewhere
Came from someone

Be a detective
Pick up on the clues
Investigate your own thoughts
Use a magnifying glass on your own behavior
Follow the trail to the beginning of your belief system

It will lead somewhere
You will uncover
Be ready to discover
You will unmask villains who were only hurt civilians

Be bold when unlocking the door to the mystery of you

Made of fire
Beyond any desire

She didn't give up easily.
Her persistence was impeccable.
The consistency of her craft was cunning.
She was determined to give herself exactly what she deserved.
She knew how to be kind to a world of hurt.
She smiled because she knew that even with all this madness going on, she had hope.
The kind of hope that could withstand any hurricane.
She was mesmerized by every mountain and miracle in her life.
She welcomed joy into her home every night and received the anointing of abundance.
Every move she made was magnanimous.
Her poise was prolific.
There was no one quite like her.
She was born to be a legend.

Who are you when no one is around?

Who are you without your appearance?
Who are you without your accomplishments?
Who are you without your income?
Who are you without your skills?
Who are you without the lifestyle you've curated?
Dissolve the walls.
What does the real you look like without anything at all?

What a privilege they say
To be pretty
To be watched but not seen
To be consumed but not valued
To be infatuated with the mere idea of you
But resistant towards any originality you hold

What a privilege they say
To be pretty

To lose yourself in the lost souls
who chase their need to be repaired
By what they see in you

My life's mission is for
Little girls to know they are powerful
For them to know of their irreplaceable presence

Powerful girl privilege
That is my promise

Some days

My body aches
My eyes swell

But my spirit carries on

I have been so many women
Where do I begin
I have been a mother, a sister, and a friend
I have been the ferocious woman whipping her hair
while dancing on a pole
I have been the woman who prefers to stay in to read
or take a stroll
I have been the woman who protects
I have been the woman who interjects
I have been the woman who is screaming to be heard
I have been the woman who doesn't say a word
I have been the woman who is hurting
I have been the woman who is singing

So when I see a woman
I am humbled in dignity
I have a deep respect
For all the different kinds
of women
in me

I wasn't interested in being used as something to check
Off your list
I am not here to fill your emptiness
I am not here to feed your ego

I will starve you
I will purge you of everything you thought was real

I am not here for your ideas of me
I am not here to romanticize
Fuck your fantasy

Mami mariposa
La diosa poderosa
Tú eres la medicina
del mundo

My toes melt into the sand
With a book in my hand
I look over to my right
I see a ripen topless woman
Hair untamed
Skin brown like the earth
Her stretch marks spread across her thighs
Like roots

Hips rollin to reggae
Laughing
Eating a mango as she wanders into the ocean

In that moment
I had never seen anyone so glorious
Her scent of freedom carried me into another dimension
Preparing me for my own ascension

When people ask what I aspire to be
I think of her

We are exhilarated at
the complexion of perceived perfection
We rush into connection
Thinking we found someone to validate
Someone to show us the direction

At the first sight of humanity
We run
Their light starts to fade out
As we look for a way out

We reject our own humanity
We block out the part
of us
We don't want to see

We have been taught
Cardboard sunsets
Barbie dream houses
with plastered smiles
All while missing the true development
of a connection worthwhile

Give me messy
Give me imperfect
Give me crazy

And I will give you fucking gold.

When our forests are on fire
When innocent life is paying the price
For every deed of greed and vice
Of those who rule and live in strife

When you feel helpless
Small, insignificant
Like nothing will ever change

Hold hands with hope
Lean into boundless belief
Activate with action

Your choices are the tipping point
Of this new earth
Kindling the flame for transformation
Stirring up the need for reformation

You play a fundamental part
You are the start of the change
You so passionately want to see

Woman
Stop looking for a lover to follow
You are meant to lead
To this day
You give life
You lead life
You do not need them in the way they need you
It is time you return to your universal knowing that
You are absolute

So often we associate enthusiasm with naivety.
As if we should be conditioned and comfortable in this reality.
As if every single day of our waking lives isn't meant to be lived in complete fascination of our existence.

Do my soft thighs make you curl your lip?
Does the length of my skirt make you pull your husband closer to your hip?
Does my youthful body make you feel diminished?
Like your life is finished?
Who robbed you of your own love?
Who said that your beauty had an expiration date?
Who said this was all you had to offer?
Who said your aging body isn't something to celebrate?

Tell me, middle-aged mothers
What can I do?
How can I be of service to you?
How can I make you see the importance in what you do?
How can I spread scriptures of the work you so selflessly commit to?

A woman's woman

She will

Look you in the eyes
Hold your hand
& want nothing more than
To be a honest sister in your life

She will uplift you
She will be stern in her stance
When holding a mirror to your face
So you remember you have a gift, too

She will help you fight all your little insecurities
She's sharp enough to know the games being played
She knows patriarchy has run its course
There is no room for competition when collaboration is her driving force

She holds her bonds close
She is loyal to the bone
If you need her
You can always pick up the phone

She inspires you to define success on your own

And see—she does this mind-boggling thing
Where she teaches you everything you need to know
She teaches you how to be comfortable in your own skin
Just by simply being herself

Watching her
Heals every part of you
Watching her
Brings out the power in you

A woman's woman is impossible to forget
You never realized how powerful a woman could be
until the day your souls met

I don't want what is easy.
I don't want a quick fix.
I don't want a temporary hold.
I don't want to get by until I get old.

HEART ♦ OF ♦ GOLD

Whenever you feel like you cannot go on. When the heartbreak is too much to bear. Even when breathing feels like choking and you are gasping for air.

I want you to remember that you carry the strength of millions of women inside of you. Their stories solidify your strength. Their hands, holding you up. Their feet, showing you how to take a step further.

I want you to remember that you have the vitality of a thousand suns. The kind of energy that will burn you and bring you back to life.

I want you to remember that you have the wisdom of a hundred shamans. This wisdom will harmonize every shard of your soul.

All inside
that heart of yours.

You can and will get through this. I assure you. I have sent help. Your angels hear you. You will slather cool aloe on your burns. You will nurse yourself back to health, just like I taught you. And, when another woman comes crying to you in pieces, you will know exactly what to do.

It is not the beauty of society that troubles me
For we all possess this innate quality
It is the replication of profitable desirability
The masks we wear

It is the fear of looking different
It is the self-betrayal of the beauty we partake in
It is the lack of self I see when I scroll
It is the desperate desire to assimilate

It is the disease of perfection
The panic of inadequacy
Self-harm in the industry

Is this really beauty?
Does this bring joy?
Or more pain?
Are you scrolling and flipping through magazines feeling less?
Punishing yourself with disdain?

I want to see rolls
I want to see lines drawn on disproportionate faces
I want to see billboards of crooked teeth

Where did we go wrong?
When did we lose ourselves within this paradox, we call beauty?
Are we tired of the abuse?
Have we had enough of the conditioning?

I want us to heal.
I want to see real.
I want to see me in the images I see.
I want to see what kind of art
we can create when we make space
for diversity.

At the end of the day
The effort you put into your life will always show
Effort shows up everywhere
It is at every corner
It is in the buildings you pass on your morning drive
It is in the fibers of your clothing
It is in the art you see
It is in every cooperation and community

The effort is there
The effort is how much you care
The effort is how you show up
The effort is the way you never give up

Clipped my wings
So you could fly

Made them into a surfboard
So you could ride the waves

Sacrificed
Never questioning why

Inhaled your smoke
So you could get high

Smiled politely
Molded into the way I should behave
Banished my soul into a cave

But even in captivity
I swing my hips
My belly belts out a savory sing
I know what spring will bring

I cannot be tamed for too long
One day I will start to hum a new song
A regal resurrection rising at dawn

I tell the tale of the woman who escaped
The woman who got away
She who always has something to say
The woman who will never stop breaking shackles
Dropping
Breadcrumbs
Along
The
Way

I must go on
For my dreams
Are not mine to own
They are the hopes
And seeds
Of all those
Who came
Before
      me.

·· THE TALE OF THREE EYES ··

seeing through the eye of the divine

"Sometimes, I feel like God talks to me through you."

Dance
in the romance
of architecture.

Observe
all the little details
in the way people dress.

See
the way people decorate their homes
like they decorate their heart.

Feel
the pure frequency of love
in all creation.

I have been writing these words my whole life
They are my thoughts
They are my friends
They are stories that never end
They are my memories
They are my dreams
They are the clothes I wear
They are the characters I seem
I dabble
I search
I live with all and none of the care
I live my life bare

See, the thing about magic is that it has always been there—right in front of you. Seeping out of the cracks on the sidewalk. Tucked in every hinge of every doorway. All it took was your new eyes to finally see it.

What if

"Well, what if I fail miserably and everybody laughs?"
The universe responds,
In the sea of embarrassment, I have built you a raft.

"Well, what if I pick the wrong path?"
There is no wrong, you create your true path if you are
courageous enough to ask.

"Well, what if time runs out and it's too late?"
When you are living in your purpose time does not seal your fate.

"Well, what if my dreams leave me broke?"
I will drape your lack and fears in my abundance cloak.

"I need to be realistic. What if my dreams aren't real?
What if none of this is possible?"
Hush child, no more questions.
Get out of the way and let me take care of all that is destined.

I need not look anywhere else but here.

You can use everything to

Create or destroy you
To empower or cower
Learn or repeat

Currency
Consumption
Connections

You choose how you want to learn by it
How you want to use it

It can give you power
Or it can be your poison

When we learn the language of the universe,
we can hear what is being said.

The universe is always speaking to us,
and whether we know it or not,
we are always speaking back.

The real gift is to tap in,
It is to know the Divine.
The source.
The language of God.

To listen to the higher teaching in every situation.
To taste the bittersweet berries in every lesson.
To speak life into every present moment.

   To see yourself as one with all that is beautiful.

This is so much bigger than us
It is not about what they did
It is not about what they said
It is not even about them at all

It is about why they are here
The message they have for you
The lesson they are carrying

We are all walking messengers
Teaching and loving
Trying to hop over the puddles
of hurt that we never caused
Yet, still, our feet get wet

When I wake
I shoot out of bed
When I wake
The sun fills me up to the top of my head
When I wake
I sing the wind in
When I wake
The chorus of birds chime in
I wake bright n' early
I cannot miss a moment of the earth's beauty

It is less about how it looks and more about how it feels

Less about the image
More about becoming the greatness that you have the power to wield

I'm here for activating conversations with tender souls
In a place where time doesn't exist
Fully embracing each other
Chest to chest

The rhythm of our heartbeats is our language

There are teachers all around me.

The trees instruct me to stand my ground.
The wind tells me to breathe life into all I do.
Animals teach me how to howl honestly.
And, if I listen closely
Plants whisper their secrets on how to grow patiently.

My compass is in the stars
They always seem to know the way

Maybe all of this suffering was to teach me that there is no
Greater love than
The love for life
The love for self

The love for the endless journey within

When you look at a mountain, you do not look at her and try to change the size of her mounds. You do not try to sand down her rocky terrain. You take a step back to behold the vast range of alps towering over you—as if you have just stumbled upon the eighth wonder of the world.

You do not interrupt the wind as she blows. You do not control when crystal droplets of rain decide to cleanse your skin.

Now, look out into nature—from the waves to the boulders. Observe the natural order of life as she flows effortlessly.

Nature does not try, nature is.
You are nature.

Now, let the natural order of your destiny unfold.

HEART OF GOLD

It is to wake up
Every single morning
With eyes of a child
To choose to live
In the wild
Emptying yourself
The willingness to say
I don't know
Learning from the sun

You are a project
That is never done

There is a difference between
Hearing the words
Knowing the meaning
& Living the practice

"Why do you write?"

I write to wake up the human spirit inside. I write so we may live, once again. I write so we may remember how it feels to be, once again.

I write to swallow my darkness, so you may taste light.

When I say
Let's clean up the earth,
I don't just mean the wrappers lying on the street.
I mean the irritable tone you used with the store clerk.
I mean the explosive hurl of anger all over your partner for making a small mistake.
I mean the passive aggressive judgment of someone you don't know who is just trying to be a little more themselves today.
The emotional littering of when
we take out our suffering on strangers passing by.
The harm we do to the ones we love.

Let's make a vow
To clean up this world, together.

I do not know

I do not know what my life will look like in five years
I do not know what I will be doing
in the next twenty-four hours
I do not know who I will meet
that will change the course of my life forever
but
I do know
that it will be
extraordinary
nothing like I have ever seen
Because
the sun is here
the moon, stars, and planets are all here
Love is here
and I wouldn't want to be on any other journey
Because

I am here

In the end,

I want to say my life was grand.
That I was courageous enough to take a stand
In the name of all I love.
I want to say I loved as much as I inhaled.
That every time I failed, I was only paving the way to prevail.

HEART OF GOLD

I meant it when I said we never die.
Don't hold on so tightly love, it's okay to let go.

I meant it when I said a heart of gold never fades
I know it's you every time it rains.
You make the heavens cry, the grace you bestow.

Everybody knows—where you can find me.

Find me in the corner of a smile.
Find me in the warm hand of an old friend who asked to stay a little while.
Find me in the clouds, rolling around, carving shapes in the sky.
Find me among the daffodils dressing up the hills with their yellow lullabies.

I meant it when I said we never die.
Don't hold on so tightly love, it's okay to fly.

The Author

Her art is in her words. She is moved by the heart of human connection and the honest experiences of evolution. Raquel Genae Flores is of Mexican descent and is inspired by reconnecting to her roots. Through self-discovery, she is led into the exploration of the deeper world within and around us. Honoring the unfolding of her journey every step of the way. Her artistic expression spills over into many avenues of performance art & creative direction.

This is a reminder that you know
exactly what you need to do.
Your calling is clear.
It is in your heart.
It is in your potential.

Be willing to explore.
You have what you need.
Do it.

return home to the truth that you are.

Made in the USA
Columbia, SC
21 December 2020